TOUGH

LOVE

Heart and Soul Food

Claudetta Griffith

Dedication

This book is dedicated to all the women who have gone before me, are with me now, and those here after I'm physically gone from this life.

My most humble prayer is that I have done right by God, and my Ancestors are proud of the woman I've become.

I dedicate this book with the love and sincerest gratitude to my grandmother, Selma Young Harris, my mother, Sheila H. Rhaburn, my godmother, Jenrine Anderson, my aunts, Dess, Eula, Lisa, Ruth, Addie, Gayle, and Harriet, my beautiful children, Brandis A. Turner, Marcus S. Hendricks, and my sisters Rondella D. Houston and a.k.a my big baby, Latricia S. Riley (A-1 since day 1).

I love you all very much.

I love music and how it speaks to my soul. The way I feel about a song shows up in my dance. The way I feel about people shows up in my heart. My heart speaks through love and compassion. May God bless everybody in the whole wide world.

~ Claudetta Griffith

Contents

Preface

This is not a "How to" book. This is a 'what I've recognized in my life' book. What I am sharing comes from personal experiences and observed situations. I didn't want this presented as an "end all to be all" answer to women's relationship issues book. That book is a myth (LMAO). This is also not a heterosexual book. Although the words come from that standpoint, I can only write about my life experience.

Life is about choices, opportunities, and consequences. It is everyone's choice to do as they please in life, and who am I to determine what they are? Exactly! Life is about love. I believe God put people on earth to love and care for one another. The "who" is none of my business. PERIOD! I want to share some heart and soul food I've received that has benefited me. The good, bad, indifferent, ups and downs. Ultimately, the message I want to convey is "You are not alone."

About the Author

Claudetta Griffith was born December 4, 1972, at the Cook County Hospital, Chicago, IL. She attended Burke Elementary School in 1976, attended Walter H. Dyett Middle School from 1983-1986 and graduated from Chicago's founder Jean Baptiste Pointe DuSable High School in 1990. She served in the United States Navy from 1991 until 2013. Upon retirement, she enrolled and graduated with a Bachelor's degree in Business Management from National Louis University in 2017. She currently resides in her hometown of Chicago, IL.

Acknowledgments

To my additional mentors throughout my life: my uncle, who I affectionately call Deddy, Mark A. Harris Sr., my late uncle, Charles A. Harris Jr., my high school band director, Mr. Timothy Galloway, he demanded my best and never allowed mediocrity, my teachers, Ms. Bonner (3rd grade) for being smart, classy and keeping me in check. I don't think I would've made it to middle school had you slacked up. Also, Mr. Taylor (6-8th grade) and Dr. Hamilton (9-12th grade) for teaching me to be proud of my heritage, and that I get to choose whether or not I would end up a stereotype and a statistic. Lastly, Ms. Simmons (11-12th grade) Home Economics. I especially want to thank Ms. Simmons for not giving me the .5 credit I needed to graduate with my senior class. I graduated from summer school and I learned that when you want to achieve a goal, you must work for it. It will not be handed to you.

My military family: K057 Company Commander UT2 Martha Wojciehowski (Wojo), my first supervisor in the fleet after joining the Navy MM1 Clarence Smalley (Cuda), MM1 Jonathan Pillion, MMCM Kenneth Cowen, MM1 Dennis Warn

(Mighty Mouse), MM1 Keith Sharpe, Ret RDML Patrick Hall, RDML. Jeff Ruth, CWO3 Shawn Steele, CDR. Skip Huck, CDR Brad Bittle, CDR Charlie Grassi, CDR Wayne Goveia, MMCM Mike Gwinn, HTCS Tim McPeek, MMC Knut Hoelstad, ENCM Roy Heringer, BMC Nick Broders, CMDCM Jeff Kirby, EMCS Steve Madison, ICCS John Coleman, ENCS Rick Christian, and CMDCM Leon Walker.

There are many more to name; I chose you because you chose me. You didn't "have" to; you "chose" to, and for that, I will forever be grateful. You chose to see past my tough facade, connect and believe in me when either I didn't believe in myself, no one else did, or I began to give up. You course corrected and calibrated as necessary. As I type these words with tears in my eyes, know that you helped shape the servant leader and woman I am.

Wojo- First leadership position in the Navy (Boot Camp) and demonstrated by example how to be respected as a leader without being the highest-ranking person.

Cuda- First leadership role in the Fleet (real Navy) as leading fireman. He showed me what it meant to work hard and play hard. He also showed me that my work ethic should never suffer for lack of praise/approval.

Jonathan- Had patience (I'm a slow learner), and helped me learn my rate in the Engineering Main Space (pit).

Kenneth- Recognized my work ethic and potential. He fought for me to be awarded my 1st Navy Achievement Medal.
Dennis and Keith- Recognized my abilities and sent me to my 1st specialized military school after 13 years in service.

Shawn, Skip, Brad, Charlie, Wayne, Mike, Tim, Knut, Roy, Nick, Jeff, Steve, John, and Rick- Thank you for the mentorship, and being my family. Thank you for challenging me to grow. Every one of you either placed or supported me in a leadership position to help me develop.

Now I know my military sisters might feel left out. Don't. For one, I don't have that many pages and second, you know how much you mean to me. We shared our love regularly. I didn't get to tell all the people listed above.

There is one of my military sisters that I must mention, Mrs. Trina McClarty. She bought me a book for my poetry years ago. I still have it and recently started to write again. It was lost to me for years, but my gratitude for your appreciation of my thoughts will never fade. Thank you again sis. I love you.

Leon- From the moment at the FY-12 Khaki ball when I saw you singing and dancing along with the newly pinned Chiefs, I knew you were someone I wanted to learn from. I didn't want to tell you then, because you know how some people act like groupies. I was a new check-in and was hesitant about my name being dragged through the rumor mill. I had only been a Chief for two years and had only seen a handful of Master Chiefs from my previous ship be genuinely open with us newbies. Boy, would I ever be right about you! If I didn't know you, I'm pretty sure I wouldn't be an author (not right now at least). I'd still be writing poetry in my book my sister gave me. You are a huge reason I developed as a Chief while stationed in Great Lakes. My spirit was broken and having you in my corner along with others with personalities like ours let me know that I was not alone. That will always be significant in my life. You embody what it is to be a servant leader. You are a great man and an inspiration to many. I love you and I thank you so much for everything you've taught and continue to teach me.

Introduction

If you take nothing from my words, please learn and live your life! Depending on your upbringing, from a young age, there's information coming from multiple directions as to how you should live your life. Some children have little to no experience to draw from. No matter your situation, learn to sit in your S.H.I.T (Sometimes Hurtful Internal Turmoil). The healing and positive forward momentum comes from the moment you choose to be still and listen in YOUR moment.

CHAPTER 1
Self-Mutilation

~◆◆◆◆◆◆◆◆◆◆◆~

Before you say to yourself, "This doesn't apply to me," let me start by saying self-mutilation comes in forms other than cutting. Staying in a relationship or job where you're disrespected, abused, neglected is a form as well. Loneliness can be a crippling feeling but being in a relationship for fear of being alone is not a good reason to stay. Jumping from one bad relationship to another is also a form. Another is going from job to job where you're miserable for a check. Keeping secrets is a sickness that can infect your soul. I consider that self-mutilation. What some don't understand is self-mutilators are fighters. Fighting to fit in, to be accepted, to be loved, to be treated fairly, to be heard, to be seen, to survive and to live.

I became a fighter when my father left without even recognizing it. I grew up a tomboy; even with my older brother around, I would fight his battles sometimes. I remember my mother sent him to the store one day. He comes running in the house out of breath with a torn gallon milk jug. She asked him what happened. When he said he got jumped in the alley coming home, I sprinted out the house looking to bash some heads. For as long as I can remember I've been that way. I was bullied as a child, so protecting others just came naturally.

What's difficult is when you're the warrior and have difficulties of your own. Who comes to the defense of the fighter? Oftentimes no one, because we don't say anything to anyone. I didn't want to appear as weak or incompetent. I didn't want to be judged by others, so I just dealt with the issue myself. A lot of times this fight is with the situation at hand. Other times it's with a person. Some of the fighters are the mother, father, wife, husband, CEO, girlfriend, sister, or child. Examining every role that you play in your life helps streamline your process in order for you to be your best self in every role. Unfortunately, a lot of us tend to do the bundle method. We don't have time to independently deal with all our issues, so we stuff and stow all the drama away. We have so many roles, that we carry the fight from one situation to the next without even realizing it. Every role we play should be given the respect and time to sort it out. Decide what you want, decide what you need, decide what will help you be successful in the role that you are examining, make a plan, and move forward. The fly by the seat of your pants method typically does not end well. Just saying...

This isn't to criticize; this is about becoming aware of behaviors and possible causes. When we bundle, stow away and keep our heads above water, we don't allow ourselves to fully confront the underlying issue/s that contribute to the behaviors exhibited. This is why "Sitting in your S.H.T.T" is crucial for healing and positive progress moving forward in our personal and professional lives. You need to get your footing before taking further steps. Your mind, body, and soul need time to heal. Otherwise, you put more pain and hurt in your bag and they reveal themselves in sometimes destructive ways. You can't fix what you won't face.

I'm pretty sure one of the reasons I allowed myself to be in unhealthy relationships is because I was never consistently taught or shown love from a man. My father left when I was around eight or nine. Up until that point, I felt loved without a doubt. Afterward, I was devastated. I also was abandoned by my brother around the age of 11. I believe my father's departure played a significant part in that. For me, the two most important men in my life left not only my mother but me and my little sisters alone. Therefore, I had no standard model of comparison in my life. I didn't know it at the time, but promiscuity showed up in my life as a result. I was seeking love from men through sex. Not porn star level, but too many.

For some, it may not make sense, but this is the predominant way I chose to receive affection from men. My mother instilled values in me, but I decided she didn't know what the fuck she was talking about (hindsight wears bifocals). Until I spoke with my mother as an adult, I placed some blame on her for my father leaving, only to find out he never explained it to her. The wave of shame washing over my body while hearing her words still resonated after our talk. Blaming her made it easier to continue on my sexual path of destruction. That way, I didn't have to take responsibility for my irresponsible and dangerous behavior.

I'm so grateful for our little talks over the years. It allowed us to put our cards on the table, apologize, forgive ourselves and ask forgiveness from one another. I forgave because I judged her as weak for allowing my father to leave. I judged her as weak for allowing my abuse (even though she knew nothing about it). I learned to forgive her because parenting doesn't come with a manual, and like me, she didn't know. She did the best she could with the tools she had. The fact that I needed more is not her fault. I was angry, but in order to heal I had to be honest and forgive myself for not communicating with her too.

With a lot of thought, prayer and counseling I have come to appreciate that this is my truth. No denial or escaping it. Therapy and this book helped me deal with repressed memories. Acceptance is one of the keys that helped me heal. I thank God and my ancestors for staying with me and guiding me towards acknowledgment and recovery. I am a much stronger and focused person because of it too.

You may have been violated (raped, bullied, cheated on, physically assaulted, etc.) years ago. The way we hurt ourselves is choosing to be a bag lady (Thank you, Erykah Badu). So many of us endure pains unimaginable, and due to our upbringing or examples presented, we feel we must be strong and push forward. There is no shame or blame in that, but what happens within us where the residual pain dwells? The longer we hold onto secrets, the sicker our heart and soul get. The armor we don does plenty to protect us from external pain sometimes, but the internal pain festers. When the opportunity to heal presents itself, you should take advantage. When you don't speak your secret into existence, you continue violating yourself damaging your heart and soul.

I refuse to give one mother fuckah that has violated me the glory of having that power of me ever again, therefore, I forgive, and I'll move on. I love myself enough to do that. If healing is important to me, then I have to let that go. I had to learn what my power is, how I gave it away, how to take my power back, and never give it away again. My power is my mind, body and control over it. It is also the respect I have for myself and the most intimate physical part of my being. My silence, inaction, and self-hatred gave it away. The moment I chose to take it back, my message to my abusers was: What you did is now on you because I refuse to carry that burden with me. My relationship with self-mutilation is now over. In blatant terms, you can kick these rocks barefoot in the middle of a sandstorm. Buh bye!

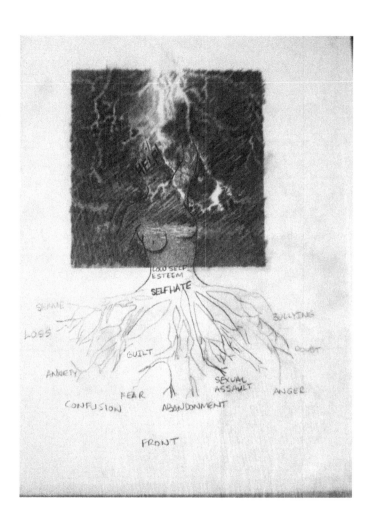

These are some of my past thoughts and feelings about my life and myself.

CHAPTER 2
Relationships

Does your lifestyle resemble your wants or needs? Let's say you want to have a $200,000 home, be married to a man who makes six figures and have two children. What exactly do you bring to the table in that equation? Let's say you want to make $75,000 a year, drive the latest luxury vehicle and you want to own a condo. What needs are being met by you in order to make sure your wants are accommodated? What is most important? The needs or the wants? I think understanding that would clear a lot of confusion in a lot of people's lives. It did for me! We need to understand what the driving force is in the way we see our lives and how they transpire.

What I saw upon reflection was I moved too quickly from initial impressions to friendships which led to a perceived state of romantic love. There wasn't enough time invested in developing a solid foundation for a relationship. I didn't know about passionate love as arousal and compassionate love as affection. I thought intense passion was a sign from the universe that our chemistry matched and that he could be or was "the one." What I learned after the fact was that passionate love is about physical and or sexual arousal and compassionate love is about trust and respect. Passionate love was heavy at the beginning of my relationships. I look back and see clear as day that it was more about sex than substance. Nothing more. Clearly nothing more than what I call a "situationship." Compassionate love has staying power. It embodies friendship, affection, durability, and honesty. My ultimate goal is compassionate love because that's a deep affectionate connection made and can endure hard times and vulnerable moments.

I've heard the word vulnerable described as weak. I've been told I'm too vulnerable. I take that as a compliment because I believe being strong means being vulnerable. It's being able to express feeling (positive/negative) in a healing way. It's laying your cards on the table and being unapologetic. Having and expressing emotions is part of human nature. It's something that I find very attractive. Now, don't get me wrong. I don't want some guy who cries non-stop. That's a bit much, but the expression of all emotions is key. One phrase that gets under my skin is "crying like a girl." What exactly does that fuckin' mean? I've learned from experience that a well-rounded man is a man I want in my corner whether that be platonic or romantic. I don't deal romantically with men who box themselves into a category. Either you display yourself to the world as you are for who you are, fully accepting, or you don't. I don't judge. I do get to choose who will remain within my circle and who does not. I have no problems with people who are flawed because I am too. What I won't do is bring a flawed person into my life without acknowledging that.

People choosing to deny imperfection are in the associate/acquaintance/friend zone. I believe this is where growth and acceptance happen. I'm not in the business of trying to repair a damaged love interest. I will befriend them though. The words 'friend' and 'family' are sacred to me. All have access, but all do not get access to my innermost thoughts. This is about trust. If a person can't accept themselves fully and be willing to do the work to grow, I can't trust that my vulnerabilities are safe with them.

Something I didn't know earlier in my life is that not receiving unconditional love from my father would affect me for the rest of my life. I also didn't know that the toll that abuse takes on a person is unrecognizable. I have since learned that my vulnerabilities affected every relationship I had as a young woman. The lessons I've learned have allowed me to grow and learn myself. After my father left at around eight or nine years old, I was sexually abused by a female family friend. Next in line were two male family members (a cousin and my brother), followed by my mother's boyfriend. I did not tell my mother about any of the abuse that I suffered during my childhood until my daughter was born and 1992. It happened because my cousin was picking my daughter up. When I witnessed this, I damn near turned into the Hulk. My memories flooded my mind and I was immediately ready to kill him! Instead, I decided there needed to be a closed-door conversation. He and I spoke in length in my mother's room. Afterward, he apologized and begged my forgiveness. I accepted his apology and immediately forgave him and haven't had an ill thought or feeling since that day. I'm pretty sure I probably wouldn't have told my mother had that not happened. I just didn't know how to talk about it. I felt dirty, ashamed, and embarrassed.

My mother demonstrated such love, compassion, strength, courage, and perseverance that she was my model to emulate whether I decided to admit it or not. After my father left, I watched her work as a Food Service Supervisor in a nursing home, a bartender at Herbs Bar in our neighborhood, and a caterer to take care of three children. She wasn't very affectionate, but instinctively I knew she loved us.

As an adult growing closer with my mother, I learned that we were more alike than I was willing to admit. There's a difference between hearing someone say something and listening to someone say something. My mother has said things to me as a teenager that I still listen to as a grown woman. As I stated, my need for male attention was horrible! My mother used to tell me "don't be so common. Just because you get called, don't mean you got to answer." I have a feeling she knew what she was doing, but I wanted it to feel as if it was my creation, as if I were the person making all this happen for me. She spoke of humble pie when I was young, but I didn't really allow it to reach the part of me that it needed to. When I was in the military I held a lot of my issues close to my chest. I thought while writing that it was because I don't trust easily. The truth is that I do! I used to be extremely naive and trusting. The real reason is I did not want people to judge me because I was ashamed. I did not understand the things that happened to me weren't my fault. I did not understand that it wasn't my responsibility to explain to anyone what happened to me. I just rejected my healing process emotionally and disrespected myself sexually.

CHAPTER 3
Sitting and Awareness

It took me a long time to understand and appreciate the full value of sitting in my S.H.I.T. (Sometimes Hurtful Internal Turmoil). I am a huge fan of honesty and genuine vulnerability. I have also fallen victim to various "lines" throughout the years. I thought I was a good judge of character. I thought that I had some sort of super science to detect genuine care and concern. Like so many others, I was naive. I thought my street sense was pretty sharp. I'd seen a few things growing up, so I underestimated my ability to fall for the okey-doke. Looking back, I realized that there were people who would say and do whatever was necessary in order to manipulate a situation, no matter the pain that ensued. I just didn't think it would happen to me, 'cuz I kept it real. I also didn't realize how that thought process allowed me to be in these ridiculous relationships. I was the victim.

I always say when you know better, you do better. That's not necessarily true because I knew some things growing up that did not materialize in my real life. Like I said, life is about choices, opportunities, and consequences. Two examples of this would be making the choice to be sexually reckless at 19 and 23 years old because the opportunity to have sex with my then-boyfriend was available to me. The consequences were pregnancies. Please don't be confused. I love and adore my children and I'm oddly grateful for the choices. All situations do not have the same end result or the same emotions that are tied to them, but as I said before, I accept my life for what it is, and I make no apologies or excuses for the choices that I have made.

As a broken woman, I have allowed myself to confuse being in love with loving the way I feel when I'm with someone. There is a huge difference. I didn't know what it took to fix the hurt or what the hurt was. This left me confused about who I was, and how I felt when I was with someone. I realized that whoever I was with soothed whatever was ailing me at the time. If I was trying to cover up some pain and I didn't want to laugh and was around a really funny man, I confused the feeling in the moment with a romantic feeling. In reality, he was funny or it was just a good fuckin' joke. Just sayin…

In my healing process, I discovered I cried far too many tears for painful situations I allowed myself to be in. There are many lessons learned. I dated at my level of self-esteem and didn't even know it was happening. My self-esteem was low! I have had a few quality men in my life, but as a broken woman, the relationship had no chance. I've been in relationships where I allowed myself to be emotionally manipulated. I allowed abusive behavior, making excuses instead of holding him accountable for his actions. I allowed my spirit to be broken. I introduced broken men into my life without first working on myself. I compared my life to other women in relationships.

Feeling less than, I allowed irresponsibility into my life for the sake of saying "I got a man." Trying to keep up a facade. My self-worth and self-esteem were in desperate need of repair. The only mechanic was me and I had to figure it out.

I'm a firm believer that people can and will do what you allow them to. It starts small. He says he's going to call and doesn't, and I say nothing. Assuming he has a legitimate reason for not keeping his word, I give him the benefit of the doubt. He disrespects me, and I don't nip it in the bud. That's giving permission for the behavior to continue. My actions let him know his behavior was acceptable and then get pissed when I've had enough. Crazy right? I know, but this was my truth. In my mind, I thought if I showed and expressed who I was that he would do the same. I never understood why a man would screw over a "good girl." Telling lies and manipulating conversation for the sake of a piece of ass. There were plenty of women giving it away. There were also women who didn't want a relationship. They only wanted sex. When I asked some of my brothers, they explained that a man would rather drive a car with fewer miles on it. Duly noted.

I ask myself clarifying questions and the answers are a reflection of actions, not words. I say what I see or feel. I trust and follow my gut as opposed to the past when I had gut feelings but chose to be goofy and gullible. That is what's real to me. A lie doesn't require sound. If I'm looking at a duck, I can "think" it's whatever I want. The truth is: A duck ain't a flamingo and a playboy ain't a prince charming. I lied to myself for years. I say that to say, in relationships, if your mate is an adult in age, and the behavior is immature, you're looking at a child. CALL A DUCK A DUCK!

If you don't have a template, you make your

blueprint based on others experiences or your fantasies. If you want the father of your children to have a loving relationship with them, what does your example look like? If you want children, do you or your partner possess the qualities you want your child to emulate? Far too often the explanation is not wanting children to grow up without a father. This is understandable.

This point is critical. The way that we treat our children is the way they will show themselves to the world. If we are belittling in nature when speaking to them, that will be a way they resolve conflict in their lives. They are only doing what they've been taught. In order to affect the outcome, be meticulous about the lesson plan. The lesson learned may not be identical to the lesson taught, but at least there won't be confusion as to the intent of the message.

When we are broken and bring broken men into our lives, the end result is oftentimes painful. This is why sitting and awareness are so important. You can't put a band-aid on a broken arm and expect proper healing to happen. You just end up with an infected arm without the full range of motion. This limits the full potential to be reached.

For those who wear heels, when they start hurting (personal or professional hurdles), you have choices.

Keep them on (stay in the relationship a.k.a stay with the situation = victimize yourself).

Change into your slippers/sandals/flip-flops/ kicks (compromise and decide to be comfortable).

Find a pair that you can be comfortable in (confront and acknowledge reality deciding to be comfortable) that fit your style = empower yourself.

When you find a pair that compliments you, your decision is about more than comfort. It's about facing a situation causing you pain and deciding that it doesn't have to be this way. You can be sexy, sassy, etc. without a missed step. Whether it's realized or not, it takes strength and courage to look at all of our life choices, analyze them and make a plan to improve the situation.

As women, sometimes we think that being strong is doing what we got to do to get through different situations in our lives. This is a fact; however, I've learned that my mental strength is equally important to my emotional strength to combat the struggles in my life. I watched my mother demonstrate acceptance, remarkable emotional and mental strength along with my baby sister. March 9th, 2016, she received the stage four pancreatic cancer diagnosis. God called her on March 21st, 2016, one week prior to her 72nd birthday.

Although this may have happened in her moment alone, not once did I witness her weep or get frustrated. Instead, she used the time she had left to give love and say her goodbyes. She also gave instructions to various family members as she was the matriarch for our family. She was and continues to be an example for me to follow. I believe from the moment her physical form departed, something changed within me. I didn't recognize it because I was lost in my black hole of grief. When I came out of it I felt myself changing. I remember her words and seek her counsel to this day.

After my marriage ended, I had to be strong and learn how to make realistic plans for my life. Working without a plan in the past was destructive and painful. It's amazing the clarity that came after. Hindsight is 20/20, right? When an entrepreneur or a corporation wants to start a business, they need to develop a business plan. Let's say they start off wanting to only sell a clothing line. The business plan or model is based on just a clothing line. Now fast forward; business is booming two years later and they want to incorporate shoes and accessories.

The same business plan for a clothing line does not accommodate the shoes and accessories, so, therefore, they have to revise the business plan. It is a fluid document. That's the best way that I can describe making a plan for my life was to accept the fact that this is not a plan set in stone. I would have to change the plan as my life changed. This is a great thing because if my life is blossoming into what I aspire it to be, that means that I'm making some of the right decisions to move on with my life. For a long time that did not happen. For a long time, my lack of direction a.k.a no business plan, meant my life sucked and remained destructively stagnant with a series of bad relationships. This is to include the time between relationships. I was celibate for almost three years and started up the same shit! The same destructive behavior with the same results with complete confusion as to why. This happened because I didn't take that honest look at myself in the mirror. I'm not talking about when you wake up, wash your face, brush your teeth, or put on makeup, etc. I'm talking about the look where you take a moment to analyze yourself and ask the question, 'Am I happy?' Are my needs being met?' When you don't do that, then you get what you get!

I sent out into the universe a hot ass mess and what I received was more volcanic lava. Until I decided to make a positive change after looking at myself and saying, "You know what? You are fucking damaged! You have some great qualities, however, you have issues we need to work on, 'cuz this is the cycle of insanity. Until I did that, nothing changed. I had settled in the past. I made excuses for myself and the men who didn't hit the mark.

With every excuse made, I made myself smaller. I chipped away at my self-worth, and self-esteem without even recognizing it. I am currently single; I don't want to be. I don't regret taking the time to learn what I want for my life. Since asking myself some honest questions, I learned that although I am not excited about being single, I don't fear being alone. This is something I've never been able to admit to in the past. In the past, by comparing my life and measuring my worth based on other women, I created the fear. As people change, so do relationships.

I've made a change within myself. The result is a change in my relationship status. It's a great step in the direction that has brought a wealth of happiness that I've never experienced. The key difference I've noticed is that my thoughts about myself and what I want have changed. Since asking myself some hard questions, I've discovered I was the start of the responsibility for my past pain. It was difficult to accept that I didn't value myself enough to demand respect. It was difficult to accept that I failed to take advantage of the resources available to me because of fear. It was also comforting to now understand that I didn't have the proper coping mechanisms.

I have made a commitment to myself to never settle or compromise myself that way ever again. Bottom line: When you start peeling back the layers of your onion and you don't like the smell, do something about it. Ask the hard questions. The answers will tell you what you need to do. You gotta LISTEN though. Don't just hear... I heard a lot of things in life. The information that stuck is the stuff I actually listened to.

CHAPTER 4
Moving Forward

In order to take new steps, I had to be fully open. I had to reconcile the fact that I had led two separate lives. One was profound and one was pathetic. The depth of my thoughts did not accurately portray the shallow life I'd lived. Once I chose to live my words, then I was moving forward in a positive direction. I have no plans on turning back either. Confronting my flaws and fears has given me a level of confidence only faked in the past. I feel much more emotionally healthier as a result.

We have this one life. It's our responsibility to do what's necessary to ensure it blossoms into the hopes and dreams we have. No matter the situation. We're responsible and accountable for our success and failure. There are people who choose to support us, but remember, the person ultimately accountable is you. Not parents, teachers, coaches, counselors, politicians, pets, or friends. Send out what you expect to receive into the universe. Reciprocity should be expected.

Pay attention to the signals you send and receive. When something is off, analyze it. If a correction is in order, make the correction. That can happen through recognition, conversation, a specific apology for the wrong, acceptance and forgiveness. When you've committed the wrong, you may not always receive forgiveness when asked. The important thing to remember is that you sincerely ask for it. Now forgive yourself and move on.

Poetry

You Gotta Love You

When the frustrations of this cold world get you down
Hold your head up girl; don't carry a frown
Sometimes it may seem that you've lost your way
Cause the demons 'round the corner tryin' to lead you astray
You gotta just "keep on keepin on" as the elders say
The sun's comin' out tomorrow; it'll be a brighter day
Don't carry the troubles of this world upon your heart
You ain't in that weight class; you can't play that part
Take one step at a time; that's all you can do
One stride after another, stay focused you'll get through
This is just some advice from one sister to another
All you need is willpower, strength and the support of another
For every successful man, there is a woman full of pride
For every ambitious woman, there is a courageous brother who is dignified
A few words of wisdom I choose to pass along

Pick that chin up! Show 'em that smile! Keep the faith; you won't go wrong
When opportunity knocks, don't be afraid. Let it in!
With a personality like yours, I know you're gonna win!
With God on high, fam by my side and belief in myself
I'll throw that doubt and self-pity high on the shelf!
Not saying you don't need nobody; that would sho'nuff be a lie
'Cuz we all need someone or something to survive
Not to give us or feed us, we can do that on our own
But to believe when no one else will to give the strength to go on
This road's so rough and weary you feel you need a 4 x 4
Because your shoes can't always get you over the hills you want to explore
I'll never lose what's deep inside that took so long to see
That I am a beautiful black butterfly for all the world to see

You gotta love you

~Claudetta Griffith

He can look into your eyes and read your soul
Though the stories he may find stay locked inside
never to be told
He understands you better than most people you
know
He shows his soul and uses it as a tool for you
both to grow
Together you're strong; divided you're lost,
forever without a clue
This truth is what keeps the union of your love,
lasting through and through
He knows your needs, fulfilled your dreams; your
happiness is what counts
Your birthright made you a queen, therefore you
will never dismount
Upon the throne, you sit because after all, it's
where you belong
He'll soothe your mind, your fears caressed, then
serenade you with song
He'll defend your honor, whenever wherever and
see you no harm done
And until you say "be on your way" to you, his
heart is won
Your love is envied by all who see it and know it
to be true
Let me tell you sumthin' young men and women,
pay attention don't misconstrue...
It's understood that life is a gift, and to take it for

granted would be a shame

If there's a moment that falls out of place, better believe there's no one to blame

Swallowing pride and admitting he's wrong sometimes can be a pain

But he knows being a fool and losing you would be the real strain

Your struggle is his, like a mirror he feels the same

The storm is somehow weathered, and you're thankful for the rain

Bring it on I say! Let's test these waves

Our commitment is like a battleship, so our love is forever saved

Whatever this world's dishin', we can go fishin'

We guaranteed to have a fry

Can you feel me? 'Cuz this lyricism is real! Never ever thought of as a lie

I preach and try to teach this 'cuz quitting on peace and love just ain't my thang

For those who think my thoughts are naive and shallow, chill... you might wanna hang

Open up, lay back, feel this vibe I'm sendin'

It ain't your body but your mind I'm befriendin'

I know someone is asking who? and what? Is he far or near?

This he could be, right next to me; Listen, I'll try to be clear

Know this my friend, I said it once; since you asked, I'll say it again
This indeed for me can only be none other than

A m-a-n

~ Claudetta Griffith

Sometimes I think we try to answer the questions that we have in our heads. What we should be doing is asking those questions to the people themselves. Who better to provide the clarity we seek than the person that has the answer? Assumptions are formed based on our answers as opposed to the truth. This further perpetuates that cycle of dysfunctional abuse in our lives. Fear of rejection sometimes prevents us from asking the tough questions. Better to hear the painful truth than a comforting lie. Less pain and time wasted on a relationship with zero potential. Some key factors in the construction of a long-lasting relationship:

* Friendship
* Loyalty
* Humor
* Trust

* Effective Communication
* Respect
* Reliability
* Intimacy

Factors which contribute to the endurance of any relationship whether it be platonic or romantic.

While physical attributes and initial impressions may light the flame for a new romance, due diligence is required to sustain it. Just like a contractor building a home or a building; without sound decision making, a strong foundation and regular maintenance, one can expect many crises and damage in the future.

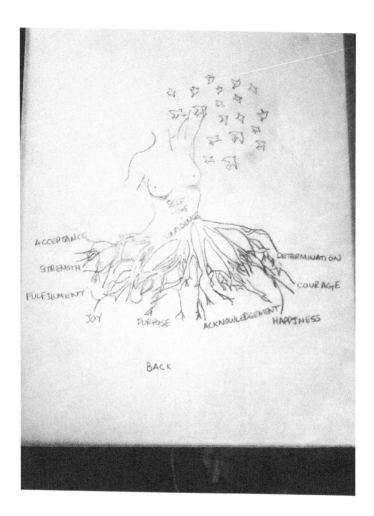

These are my thoughts after my healing with regards to my life and the joy I feel within.

CHAPTER 5
20 questions to ponder

Does your significant other ever ask you these questions?

1. How do you feel?

If a person isn't concerned with how you feel, why are they with you? I can count the relationships on one hand when I was asked this question. I didn't realize the importance at the time, but by not being asked, it showed me the lack of concern for my well-being.

2. What do you need?

This deals with their interest in providing support and interest in you achieving your goals. I didn't see that it's deeper than upcoming bills, work deadlines, etc. I got wrapped up in sexual chemistry disguised as compatibility. The question speaks to a partnership with longevity and goals (higher education, home, entrepreneurship, family, retirement, etc.).

3. How can I support or assist you?

This speaks to a union. A commitment to your success and healthy resolve. It means so much to know your loved one is in your corner fighting battles with you. The question says: I will not only be here with you, but we're in this together. The struggle is OURS! Have you ever had someone next to you, but because there's no connection, they might as well be 1,000 miles away? If you answered yes, this is a pivotal question to ask.

4. What do you want?

I used to be afraid to ask for definitive responses. Fear of rejection is the reason. I later learned that at a certain point in a relationship, one or both people come to the conclusion that they want more. When that moment presents itself, questions should be raised. Some will be ready and some won't, but you won't know unless you ASK! The obvious answers should be discounted automatically (great job, sex, friends, etc.). This question requires specificity. This is from one person to another, not an umbrella answer. If the answers are vague, that is a clear sign that you and your partner may not be on the same page. Another thing to think about is the uncomfortable conversations that may happen after. If your relationship can't survive a disagreement, how is longevity a possibility? Long-term relationships don't come free from some turbulence. Not many things worth having come easy. If the person you're in a relationship with can't endure a little pain or discomfort, that's a sign you should pay attention to.

5. What are your intentions?

Are they filling a void or genuinely interested in you?

Do you ever ask yourself these questions?

Please do not let fear of rejection keep you from asking this question. The wrong person you're asking could be blocking the right person's access to you.

6. Does their behavior align with their words?

When I was a child, I wanted to be a teacher or lawyer. I also did nothing growing up to put me on either of those paths. End result: I did not become a teacher or lawyer. Words without action = ideas or thoughts. Both are nice, but ineffective without an executed plan. If the walk doesn't match the talk, it's probably bull shit.

7. What do I bring to the table?

Being realistic and clear on your contribution can help provide focus on what you look for in a partner.

8. What are my expectations from my partner?

It's very important to know what your standards are. I always had expectations in my head, but not my mouth. If you don't speak it, you walk blind and volunteer yourself to be victimized as I did. Know what you want and enter relationships with that laid out on the table. Your partner can't be held accountable for standards not met that weren't set.

9. How do I want to be treated?

Do you want peasant, friend, friends with benefits, or royal treatment? You carry and present yourself the way you want to be treated. There will be those who see what they want to see, but after you make your presence felt, people have no excuse for treating you differently. The key is knowing who you are and what you're willing to allow in your life. You can't reasonably expect the royal treatment while conducting yourself as a peasant.

10. What are my expectations from this relationship?

Are you thinking short- term (boyfriend/girlfriend), or long-term (marriage)? For a lot of people, they can sum up the length of a relationship within the first six months based on chemistry and interactions with the person.

11. Who am I?

If you can't answer this question for yourself, how can you present yourself to a partner, and who are you presenting to the world?

12. What do I want?

If you don't know, how do you know what to look for in a love interest? Self-preservation is more than harm or death to me. It's about ownership of your path in life. Everyone has the divine right to dream big and make plans for that to come true. Everyone in your life may not agree or support your goals, but that is fine. That should not stop you from deciding what you want for and in your life. Self-preservation is about more than protection from harm or death to me.

13. What are my strengths?

It's important to know what you bring to the table. This table can be in a dining room or a boardroom.

14. What are my weaknesses?

Not acknowledging that there is room to grow will stunt your personal and professional progress. We all have things to work on. From the oldest to the youngest, from the most to the least educated, from the richest to the poorest, no one is without flaws.

15. What are my goals?

Do you want to own your own business? Do you want to graduate? Do you want to be the associate manager at your job? Do you want zero or anywhere from two to five kids? Do you want to own your own home in five years? Do you want to gain/lose three pounds? When you're in a relationship, these things should be discussed.

16. What makes me happy?

Is it live concerts? Walks in the park? The beach? Shopping? Helping others? Writing? Singing? Warm baths? Know this. Getting to know yourself answers this question. A lot of the time, people spend time and energy bringing happiness to another person without realizing they don't even like the activity. When times get rough, it becomes a sore subject to throw in the other person's face. When you know what makes you happy, when you meet someone and discuss these things, it's all laid out. No surprises.

17. Who do I want to be?

The mirror tells no lies. We do, but it never does. The mirror provides the clarity needed to gain focus moving forward.

18. How do I feel when I say no to something/someone?

Are you sad, or glad? Appreciating the beauty in the word 'no' brings a sense of calm I can't describe. Understanding your limitations and placing priority on events and people in your life is amazing. Saying no with no malice in my heart is one of the most respectful things I can do. It is a way of understanding the power and forgiveness in owning my choice.

19. What am I willing to compromise?

Sometimes there are deal breakers and there are issues we simply don't like. There is a difference and you must know that. It's important to know the flexible issues to avoid unnecessary disagreements. There were times when I compromised my morals and my integrity to be what someone else wanted me to be personally and professionally. I shrunk.

20. What top qualities must I light up about in a partner?

This answer prevents settling.

Never forget:

Forever could mean four hours, eight weeks, six years or 50 years. The foundation and work throughout the relationship will determine the length.

You are enough. Have faith in that and know that you can't "make" someone get that. That's not your responsibility. Your responsibility lies in walking in your truth, showing up in your life, and letting it speak volumes to the world.

Doing something wrong without knowledge is a mistake.

Making a conscious choice to do something wrong having a full understanding of the ramifications is wrong, and disrespectful. FLAT OUT!

Take pride in who you are and where you come from.
Appreciate the negative and positive.
Embrace the lessons learned.

On this journey, the times get hard.

So hard, you may not feel as if you have the strength to overcome the past, the courage to face the future or the wisdom to make the right decisions.

The answer is in your heart.

The heart is a strong organ and with a little help from your brain,

the path you walk will lead to happiness and prosperity.

Time brings about change.

Change brings about knowledge.

Knowledge enhances understanding.

Understanding gives insight in order to obtain wisdom.

Wisdom… Wisdom empowers and enriches the soul.

~ Claudetta Griffith

1987 High School

1st All City Band Performance 1987

ROTC 1988

Pom-Pom Team 1989

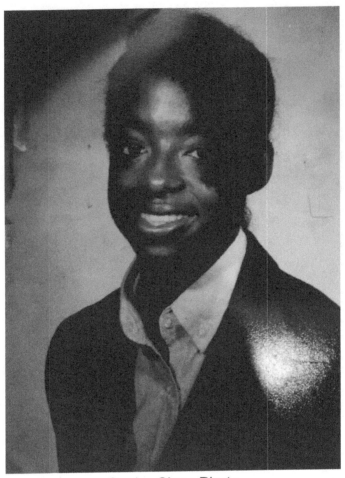

Senior Class Photo

Boot Camp Photo
(We were told to give one smiling and one
serious. Apparently, my smile wasn't that good.
LOL!)

Post Boot Camp Graduation
(After I returned home in 1991)

Basic Engineering Skills Graduation 1991

MM1 CLAUDETTA RHABURN

Deployment 2008

2011

2012

2013

2014

2016

Claudetta Griffith

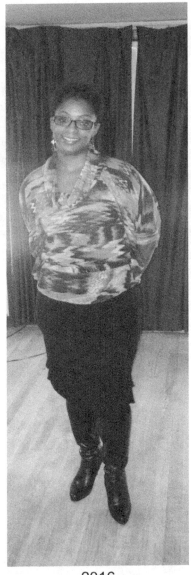

2016

2018

2018

2018

2018

2018

With nearly every photo you see, I was in some form of pain (psychological, physical, emotional etc). Especially the photos prior to 2011. I was unaware just how much damage had been done. I was also unaware of the part I played. I chose for many years to hide it beneath my smile. I learned to compartmentalize my emotions in the military, because the mission always came first. Don't be confused. I was genuinely happy in every moment, all the while suffering within.

A song I love "Smile" written by Charles Chaplin, John Turner, and Gregory Parsons and sung by Nat King Cole comes to mind. Although I disagree with the lyric "Smile, what's the use of crying", I completely strive to live this way.

My belief is that I understand the sentiment behind the lyric, but I also believe a good cry every now and again cleanses the spirit and lifts some of the emotional burden carried.

I have smiled in spite of immense trauma. I wish for others to do the same, but at the same time seek answers to the why. Why am I sad? Why am I mad? Why am I disgusted? Why do I feel ashamed? Why does it hurt so bad?

Peel back the layers of the onion and just cry. Cry and ask those ugly questions to get the answers to prevent that pain from ever happening again. It can be a painful, yet beautiful start.

That way, there's healing in your joy. Not just you wearing a mask.

Thank you for giving your time and attention to my thoughts. I greatly appreciate it.

,

Made in the USA
Coppell, TX
09 June 2020

27400407R00052